Playlist for the Apocalypse

Also by Rita Dove

Collected Poems: 1974–2004

The Penguin Anthology of Twentieth-Century American Poetry (editor)

Sonata Mulattica (poems)

American Smooth (poems)

On the Bus with Rosa Parks (poems)

The Poet's World (essays)

Mother Love (poems)

The Darker Face of the Earth (verse drama)

Selected Poems

Through the Ivory Gate (novel)

Grace Notes (poems)

Thomas and Beulah (poems)

Fifth Sunday (short stories)

Museum (poems)

The Yellow House on the Corner (poems)

Playlist

for the

APOCALYPSE

Poems

Rita Dove

W. W. NORTON & COMPANY
Independent Publishers Since 1923

For information about permission to reproduce selections from this book,
write to Permissions, W. W. Norton & Company, Inc.,
500 Fifth Avenue, New York, NY 10110

For information about special discounts for bulk purchases, please contact
W. W. Norton Special Sales at specialsales@wwnorton.com or 800-233-4830

Manufacturing by BVG Fairfield
Book design by Daniel Lagin
Production manager: Julia Druskin

Library of Congress Cataloging-in-Publication Data

Names: Dove, Rita, author.
Title: Playlist for the Apocalypse : poems / Rita Dove.
Description: First edition. | New York, NY : W. W. Norton & Company, [2021]
Identifiers: LCCN 2021011714 | ISBN 9780393867770 (hardcover) |
ISBN 9780393867787 (epub)
Subjects: LCGFT: Poetry.
Classification: LCC PS3554.O884 P58 2021 | DDC 811/.54—dc23
LC record available at https://lccn.loc.gov/2021011714

W. W. Norton & Company, Inc., 500 Fifth Avenue, New York, N.Y. 10110
www.wwnorton.com

W. W. Norton & Company Ltd., 15 Carlisle Street, London W1D 3BS

1 2 3 4 5 6 7 8 9 0

in memory of my parents

Contents

Spring Cricket

A Standing Witness

Eight Angry Odes

Little Book of Woe

Playlist for the Apocalypse

Prose in a Small Space

It's supposed to be prose if it runs on and on, isn't it? All those words, too many to fall into rank and file, stumbling bare-assed drunk onto the field reporting for duty, yessir, spilling out as shamelessly as the glut from a megabillion-dollar chemical facility, just the amount of glittering effluvium it takes to transport a little girl across a room, beige carpet thick under her oxfords, curtains blowzy with spring—is that the scent of daffodils drifting in?

Daffodils don't smell but prose doesn't care. Prose likes to hear itself talk; prose is development and denouement, anticipation hovering near the canapés, lust rampant in the antipasto—e.g., a silver fork fingered sadly as the heroine crumples a linen napkin in her lap to keep from crying out at the sight of Lord Campion's regal brow inclined tenderly toward the wealthy young widow . . . prose applauds such syntactical dalliances.

Then is it poetry if it's confined? Trembling along its axis, a flagpole come alive in high wind, flapping its radiant sleeve for attention—*Over here! It's me!*—while the white spaces (air, field, early morning silence before the school bell) shape themselves around that one bright seizure . . . and if that's so what do we have here, a dream or three paragraphs? We have white space too; is this music? As for all the words left out, banging at the gates . . . we could let them in, but where would we go with our orders, our stuttering pride?

Time's Arrow

Who is it that can tell me who I am?

—*Shakespeare*, King Lear

You blows who you is.

—*Louis Armstrong*

There are notes between notes, you know.

—*Sarah Vaughan*

Bellringer

I am as true to that bell as to my God.
Henry Martin

I was given a name, it came out of a book—
I don't know which. I've been told the Great Man
could recite every title in order on its shelf.
Well, I was born, and that's a good thing,
although I arrived on the day of his passing,

a day on which our country fell into mourning.
This I heard over and over, from professors
to farmers, even duel-scarred students;
sometimes, in grand company, remarked upon
in third person—a pretty way of saying

more than two men in a room means the third
can be ignored, as I was when they spoke
of my birth and Mr. Jefferson's death
in one breath, voices dusted with wonderment,
faint sunlight quivering on a hidden breeze.

I listen in on the lectures whenever I can,
holding still until I disappear beyond third person—
and what I hear sounds right enough;
it eases my mind. I know my appearance
frightens some of the boys—the high cheeks

and freckles and not-quite-Negro eyes
flaring gray as storm-washed skies
back home; it shames them to be reminded.
So much for book learning! I nod
as if to say: *Uncle Henry at your service,*

then continue on my way through darkness
to start the day. This is my place:
stone rookery perched above
the citadels of knowledge,
alone with the bats and my bell,

keeping time. Up here, molten glory
brims until my head's rinsed clear.
I am no longer *a dreadful coincidence*
nor debt crossed off in a dead man's ledger;
I am not summoned, dismissed—

I am the clock's keeper. I ring in their ears.
And every hour, down in that
shining, blistered republic,
someone will pause to whisper
Henry!—and for a moment

my name flies free.

Lucille, Post-Operative Years

Most often she couldn't
think—which is to say she thought of
everything, and at once—
catfish in the bathtub, a bowl of oatmeal
nailed with a butter square,
her disappointment
palpable as bread.

Then, sudden as a wince,
she couldn't remember a thing.
So she got out the broom and swept
the back porch,
that anonymous, hoodwinked sea. . . .

What bothered her: the gaps
between. Her first camisole,
then this morning's scalding coffee.
How men became themselves while playing cards.
How women became themselves while sleeping.

When she was young she used to sit
in the very top of the plum tree.
She swept on until
she heard Mama whispering
Hush chile, time's a-wastin'
—dry leaf in the palm, dry leaf on the branch—
and the porch was clean.

Family Reunion

Thirty seconds into the barbecue,
my Cleveland cousins
have everyone speaking
Southern—broadened vowels
and dropped consonants,
whoops and caws.
It's more osmosis than magic,
a sliding thrall back to a time
when working the tire factories
meant entire neighborhoods coming
up from Georgia or Tennessee,
accents helplessly intact—
while their children, inflections flattened
to match the field they thought
they were playing on, knew
without asking when it was safe
to roll out a drawl . . . just as

it's understood "potluck" means
resurrecting the food
we've abandoned along the way
for the sake of sleeker thighs.
I look over the yard to the porch
with its battalion of aunts,
the wavering ranks of uncles
at the grill; everywhere else
hordes of progeny are swirling
and my cousins yakking on
as if they were waist-deep in quicksand
but like the books recommend aren't moving
until someone hauls them free—

Who are all these children?
Who had them, and with whom?
Through the general coffee tones
the shamed genetics cut a creamy swath.
Cherokee's burnt umber transposed
onto generous lips, a glance flares gray
above the crushed nose we label
Anonymous African: It's all here,
the beautiful geometry of Mendel's peas
and their grim logic—

and though we remain
clearly divided on the merits
of okra, there's still time
to demolish the cheese grits
and tear into slow-cooked ribs
so tender, we agree they're worth
the extra pound or two
our menfolk swear will always
bring them home. Pity
the poor soul who lives
a life without butter—
those pinched knees
and tennis shoulders
and hatchety smiles!

Girls on the Town, 1946

(Elvira H. D., 1924–2019)

You love a red lip. The dimples are
extra currency, though you take care to keep
powder from caking those charmed valleys.
Mascara: Check. Blush? Oh, yes.
And a hat is never wrong
except evenings in the clubs: There
a deeper ruby and smoldering eye
will do the trick, with tiny embellishments—
a ribbon or jewel, perhaps a flower—
if one is feeling especially flirty or sad.

Until Rosie fired up her rivets, flaunting
was a male prerogative; now, you and your girls
have lacquered up and pinned on your tailfeathers,
fit to sally forth and trample each plopped heart
quivering at the tips of your patent-leather
Mary Janes. This is the only power you hold onto,
ripped from the dreams none of you believe
are worth the telling. Instead of mumbling,
why not decorate? Even in dim light
how you glister, sloe-eyed, your smile in flames.

Eurydice, Turning

Each evening I call home and my brother answers.
Each evening my rote patter, his unfailing cheer—
until he swivels; leans in, louder:

"It's your daughter, Mom! Want to say
hello to Rita?" My surprise each time
that he still asks, believes in asking.

"Hello, Rita." A good day, then;
the voice as fresh as I remember.
I close my eyes to savor it

but don't need the dark to see her
younger than my daughter now,
wasp-waisted in her home-sewn coral satin

with all of Bebop yet to boogie through.
No wonder Orpheus, when he heard
the voice he'd played his lyre for

in the only season of his life that mattered,
could not believe she was anything
but who she'd always been to him, for him. . . .

Silence, open air. I know what's coming,
wait for my brother's "OK, now say
goodbye, Mom"—and her parroted reply:

"Goodbye, Mom."
That lucid, ghastly singing.
I put myself back into a trance

and keep talking: weather, gossip, news.

Scarf

Whoever claims beauty
lies in the eye
of the beholder

has forgotten the music
silk makes settling
across a bared

neck: skin never touched
so gently except
by a child

or a lover.

From the Sidelines

It seems I have always sat here watching men like you—
who turn heads, whose gaze is either a kiss
or a slap or the whiplash of pure disregard. Why fret? All
you're doing is walking. You're this year's *It*, the
one righteous integer of cool cruising down a great-lipped
channel of hushed adoration, women turned girls
again, brightening in spite of themselves. That
brave, wilting smile—you don't see it, do you?
How she tells herself to move on; blinks until she can.

Mirror

Mirror,   Mirror,
take this   this take
from   from
me: me:
my blasted gaze,   gaze blasted, my
sunken   sunken
astonishment. Resolve   resolve, astonishment.
memory & rebuild; shame'll   Shame'll rebuild & memory
dissolve   dissolve
under powder pressed into   into pressed powder under
my skin.   skin, my

Oh, avalanche, my harbor: harbor, my avalanche. Oh
can I   I can
look   look
over you,   you over,
pit & pustule, crease & blotch,   blotch & crease, pustule & pit—
without seeing   seeing without
you through you—   you, through you.
if all I am   Am I all if
(Am I all?)   all I am
is *Woe is*   is *Woe is*
me?   *me?*

Found Sonnet: The Wig

100% human hair, natural; Yaki synthetic, Brazilian blend,
Malaysian, Kanekalon, Peruvian Virgin, Pure Indian;
iron-friendly, heat-resistant; bounce, volume, featherweight,
Short 'n' Sassy, Swirls & Twirls, Smooth & Sleek and Sleek & Straight,

Wet and Wavy, Futura fibre, weave-a-wig or Shake-n-Go;
classic, trendy, micro-kink; frosted pixie, tight cornrow;
full, three-quarter, half, stretch cap, drawstring, ear tabs, combs;
chignon, headband, clip-in bangs; easy extensions and ponytail
                                                                domes—

long or bobbed, hand-tied, layered, deep twist bulk, prestyled updo,
Remi closure, Swiss lace front, invisible L part, J part, U;
feathered, fringed, extended neck; tousled, spiky, loose cascades,
sideswept, flipped ends, corkscrews, spirals, Rasta dreads, Ghana
                                                                braids;

Passion Wave, Silk Straight, Faux Mohawk, Nubian locks, Noble Curl:
Cleopatra, Vintage Vixen, Empress, Hera, Party Girl.

Trans-

I work a lot and live far less than I
could, but the moon is beautiful and
there are blue stars . . . . I live the
chaste song of my heart.

Federico García Lorca to Emilia Llanos Medina

Nov 25, 1920

The moon is in doubt
over whether to be
a man or a woman.

There've been rumors,
all manner of allegations,
bold claims and public lies:

He's belligerent. She's in a funk.
When he fades, the world teeters.
When she burgeons, crime blossoms.

O how the operatic impulse wavers!
Dip deep, my darling, into the blank pool.

Climacteric

I look around and suddenly all my friends have flown:
gone shopping, on a bender, off playing cards
while stink bugs ravish their boutique vineyards,
cooing over grandkids in lieu of hugging their own

frazzled issue—who knows? They're anywhere but
here, darkening my stoop on this sun-filled, vacant day. Not that
I'd welcome their airy distraction—not as long as the pages
keep thickening as I stir, lick a finger to test the edges

(illicit snacking, calorie-free)—but I'll confess this
once: If loving every minute spent jostling syllables
while out in the world others slog through their messes
implies such shuttered industry is selfish or irresponsible,

then I'm the one who's fled. Ta-ta! I'm not ashamed;
each word caught right is a pawned memory, humbly reclaimed.

Island

A room in one's head
is for thinking
outside of the box,
though the box is still
there—cosmic cage,
Barnum's biggest, proudest Ring.
My land: a chair, four sticks
with a board laid across:
This is the raft
I pile my dreams on,
set out to sea.
Look for me, shore.

Vacation

I love the hour before takeoff,
that stretch of no time, no home
but the gray vinyl seats linked like
unfolding paper dolls. Soon we shall
be summoned to the gate, soon enough
there'll be the clumsy procedure of row numbers
and perforated stubs—but for now
I can look at these ragtag nuclear families
with their cooing and bickering
or the heeled bachelorette trying
to ignore a baby's wail and the baby's
exhausted mother waiting to be called up early
while the athlete, one monstrous hand
asleep on his duffel bag, listens,
perched like a seal trained for the plunge.
Even the lone executive
who has wandered this far into summer
with his lasered itinerary, briefcase
knocking his knees—even he
has worked for the pleasure of bearing
no more than a scrap of himself
into this hall. He'll dine out, she'll sleep late,
they'll let the sun burn them happy all morning
—a little hope, a little whimsy
before the loudspeaker blurts
and we leap up to become
Flight 828, now boarding at gate 17.

A·wing′

Die Zeit im Grund, Quinquin, die Zeit,
die ändert doch nichts an den Sachen.
Die Zeit ist ein sonderbar Ding.
Wenn man so hinlebt, ist sie rein gar nichts.
Aber dann auf einmal, da spürt man nichts als sie.

Marschallin's monologue, Der Rosenkavalier

Her noble soprano swells the car radio,
tone escalating on tone, a wine goblet
filling, then pouring out:

as frightening a perfection as the Alps
glimpsed, unguarded,
at the free end of a cobbled alley

crisscrossed with Monday's laundry,
bed sheets and towels.
We've stopped to photograph Switzerland

en route to gentler climes. At this altitude
I'm lightheaded, though I've never felt
more brunette, here among the blondes

Schwarzkopf celebrated
(despite the irony of her name, a blemish
no native speaker hears). *Strange,*

the Marschallin trills, *but time*
changes nothing, actually.
Jolted, my chest stutters,

remembers to re-inflate—
glacial sun, iodine empyrean.
I lift the lens and snap. Even this deep

into summer, snow continues to pleat
those deadly crevasses—(*Hochsommer*,
the natives call it: high, deep, black,

white)—just as she continues
to thrill us with her icy passion, her
platinum Marschallin.

There's really no end to this
perfection: It stands there
ignoring you, until you notice—and then

there's nothing else.

After Egypt

The slum is the measure of civilization.

—*Jacob Riis*

Everyone's quick to blame the alien.

—*Aeschylus*

Little Town

Cobble your streets and no whining:
Stones are abundant here,
Stones and weather and air.

Foundry

Cast out. Cast in
bronze, in iron
(medallions never),
in fervor, in torment,
testing for a nibble,
a bite of glory—
then reeled into The
Net. Always the net's
diaphanous crucible,
a seething creel
dripping with its
wretched catch.

STAND UP, JEW!
NIGGER, HALT!
RUN, FAG, RUN!
JUST TRY IT, BITCH.

I hear you. Your eyes
have screamed themselves
into slits and I am tired
beyond longing, past
caring if the stick
is thick. You think surely
there's no harm in
rounding up trash
and hauling it
to the dump where it
won't offend your delicate
snub nose. You think

as long as we stay where
you've tossed us, on
the slag heap of your regard,
the republic is safe.

OUT OF SIGHT, OUT OF MIND

Now you see me
Now you don't

Sarra's Answer

in response to a sonnet by Gabriele Zinano

You asked if I could swear this faith of mine
would guarantee to get me into heaven—
if not, then why not take the veil
and strike an iron-clad deal with God?
You wrote this in earnest, as if desire
were not a part of believing, and your zeal
one last irresistible swish of frosting
on the wafer offered up in trade for sin.
There is no way to say this sweetly: Death
will sour my breath before I set foot
inside that gilded gambler's den. Aim your hope
elsewhere: There can be no prize behind Door
Number Three grander than all I'll inherit—
passage from these lean walls into endless Room.

Sarra's Blues

I am not the one you hoped for
(it is morning my heart beats)
I am not the one you think I am
(my bed is stale the air is sweet)

I will not give in to sorrow
(though the lapping water purrs)
I will not be soothed by shadows
(I can hear the earth's low roar)

You cannot find me in these lines
(I have not gone it is too soon)
I cannot find the noblest rhymes
(I did not die this afternoon)

From wan noon into dim evening
(brackish spittle clanging skull)
Evening grims into night's easing
(water settles light decays)

What I whisper will not soothe you
(fevered washrag soured wet)
Do not look for peace or wisdom
(do remember do regret)

I have nothing left to tell you
(muffled voices fade away)
True I will not live forever
(but I shall not die today)

Aubade: The Constitutional

Leone da Modena. The Veneto

A day like this I should count
among the miracles of living—breath,

a heart that beats, that aches and sings;
even the ecstasy of thirst

or sweat peppering my brow,
fanned by the mercurial breezes

crisscrossing this reserve,
our allotment on earth—

why, then, am I unhappy

when all around me
the human pageant whirrs?

This much I can do for my lost,
my sweet and damaged tribe:

Each morning I pace the tattered verge
of their Most Serene Republic,

patrol each canal's fogged sibilance,
chanting *a day unlike all others*—

and then I count it, and the next,
God willing, and each day thereafter

as a path free of echoes,
a promise with no perimeters,

my foot soles polishing the scarred stones.

Sketch for Terezín

breathe in breathe out
that's the way

in   out
left   right

where did we leave from?
when do we stop leaving?

*

This far west, summer nights cool off
but stay light, blue-stung,
long after sleep lowers its merciful hammer.

*

breathe   left
breathe   right

one   two
in   out

*

There will be music and ice cream
and porcelain sinks.
Carts of bread for the looking;
choirs and gymnastics.

I get to carry the banner.

*

that's the way keep it up
in out   in out

where did we leave from
when did we stop leaving

*

I was a girl when I arrived,
carrying two pots
from my mother's kitchen.
It was October, growing crisp,
my sweater soft as cream cakes,
my braid blonder than the star
stitched across my heart.

*

breathe   breathe
that's the way

left right left
right left right

*

no one asks what village I'm from
though I look out from its leaf-green eyes

no one asks if I remember how the butterflies
startled, churning up lemony clouds

no one else hears the river chafing its banks
the one road singing its promises
going out

*

when did we leave from
where did we stop leaving

*

if I am to become a heavenly body
I would like to be a comet
a streak of spitfire consuming itself
before a child's upturned wonder

Orders of the Day

After the bellowed call to rise, the cold dribble wash-up
before making our cots; after chores were dealt out
as we crumbled bread into sour cabbage, then fell

in line to be totted up, numbers matched to fates;
there was a moment—before the scramble to class,
lookouts posted below the attic hutch, no more than

a flicker, a bright, brutal remembering—
when we became ourselves again,
cowlicked and plaited, flush with pocketed apples

or tucked-away sweets. We were not
hunched in rain being counted or shivering
under rafters, trying to keep pace with

our dreams of the outside world.
We were merely children. And that
brief forgetting, that raging stupor

we tried to hold quiet in our heads
as if in a brimming goblet
until the day lurched upright, barking its orders—

was either the most blissful or shattering instant
we would live through on earth:
this hard and sullen earth

we no longer recognized but would,
sooner than later, commit our souls to
when at last our bodies crumbled

into their final resting place.

Transit

If music be the food of love, play on.

This is the house that music built:
each note a fingertip's purchase,
rung upon rung laddering

across the unspeakable world.
As for those other shrill facades,
rigged-for-a-day porticos

composed to soothe regiments
of eyes, guilt-reddened,
lining the parade route

(horn flash, woodwind wail) . . .
well, let them cheer.
I won't speak judgment on

the black water passing for coffee,
white water for soup.
We supped instead each night

on Chopin, hummed our grief-
soaked lullabies to the rapture
rippling through. Let it be said

while in the midst of horror
we fed on beauty—and that,
my love, is what sustained us.

[Alice Herz-Sommer, survivor of the Theresienstadt concentration camp]

Declaration of Interdependence

Hooknose, Canada Goose, slit-eyed Toucan.
Porch monkey, baboon, trash-talking magpie.

I cover my head in adoration, just as you doff your hat.
Do not rub my head. Don't even think about it.

I bob as I chant, I pray as I breathe. Does that disgust you?
I shout to the Lord, dance out my joy. Does that
amuse you?

To my knowledge I have never terminated a deity.
Last time I looked, I did not have a tail.

Business is not "in" my blood. I attended university. I studied.
I am a trained athlete. Nothing I do on the court
is natural.

Matzo is not a culinary delicacy: There wasn't a menu.
Fried chicken will kill you just as easy as the
Colonel.

You buy tickets to hear me crack jokes about my tribe. Are you
uncomfortable yet?
Suddenly you're walking up the same street I'm
walking down. Are you frightened yet?

You laugh, and forget. I laugh, and remember.
I laugh to forget, and the thorn deepens.

Excuse me, but what do vermin actually look like?
Raccoons are intelligent, curious, and highly
industrious.

I am not the problem or even a problem. Problems have provenance;
                                        someone created them.
          I'm neither exotic nor particularly earthy. I was a
                              child once; I belonged to someone.

No, I do not know how to play the violin.
          Sorry, I'm tone-deaf. No rhythm here.

Bagel-dog, Bronx Indian, Beastie Boy.
          Buckwheat, Burr Head, banjo lips.

I have never even seen a well.
          So is *that* a poplar?

Do not talk about my mother.
          Do not talk about my mother.

Elevator Man, 1949

Not a cage but an organ:
If he thought about it, he'd go insane.
Yes, if he thought about it
philosophically,
he was a bubble of bad air
in a closed system.

He sleeps on his feet
until the bosses enter from the paths
of Research and Administration—
the same white classmates
he had helped through Organic Chemistry.
A year ago they got him a transfer
from assembly line to Corporate Headquarters,
a "kindness" he repaid

by letting out all the stops,
jostling them up and down
the scale of his bitterness
until they emerge queasy, rubbing
the backs of their necks,
feeling absolved and somehow
in need of a drink. *The secret,*

he thinks to himself, *is not
in the pipe but
the slender breath of the piper.*

Youth Sunday

16th Street Baptist Church
Birmingham, Alabama

This morning's already good—summer's
cooling, Addie chattering like a magpie—
but today we are leading the congregation.
Ain't *that* a fine thing! All in white *like angels,*
they'll be sighing when we appear at the pulpit
and proclaim "Open your hymnals—"
Addie, what's the page number again?
Never mind, it'll be posted. I think. I hope.
Hold still, Carole, or else this sash will never
sit right! There. Now you do mine.
Almost eleven. I'm ready. My, don't we look—
what's that word the Reverend used in
last Sunday's sermon? Oh, I got it: *ethereal.*

Aubade East

Harlem, a.m.

Today's the day, I can taste it.
Got my gray sweats pouting in a breeze
so soft, I feel like I'm still wrapped for sleeping
as I head uptown in my undercover power-suit,
bitch sunlight fingering the spaced-out tenements.

This morning there ain't nothing I *can't* do.
This is my territory, I know all of it—
ten long blocks flanked by mighty water.
Walking any Avenue is like riding
a cosmic surfboard on the biggest wave

of the goddam century, the East River
twerking her bedazzled behind
while sky spills coins like a luck-crazed
Vegas granny flush at the slots. Today

I'm gonna make out like a bandit myself:
hook up with my buds to drop
a few shots on the courts, ogle the ladies,
then play the rest of the day

as it comes   see where it goes
feeling good
feeling good
somewhere over the Hudson
the sun   heading home

Trayvon, Redux

It is difficult / to get the news from poems / yet men die miserably
every day / for lack / of what is found there. / Hear me out / for
I too am concerned / and every man / who wants to die at peace
in his bed / besides.

William Carlos Williams, "Asphodel, That Greeny Flower"

Move along, you don't belong here.
This is what you're thinking. Thinking
drives you nuts these days, all that
talk about rights and law abidance when
you can't even walk your own neighborhood
in peace and quiet, *get your black ass gone.*
You're thinking again. Then what?
Matlock's on TV and here you are,
vigilant, weary, exposed to the elements
on a wet winter's evening in Florida
when all's not right but no one sees it.
Where are they—the law, the enforcers
blind as a bunch of lazy bats can be,
holsters dangling from coat hooks above their desks
as they jaw the news between donuts?

Hey! It tastes good, shoving your voice
down a throat thinking only of sweetness.
Go on, choke on that. Did you say something?
Are you thinking again? Stop!—and
get your ass gone, your blackness,
that casual little red riding hood
I'm just on my way home attitude
as if this street was his to walk on.
Do you hear me talking to you? Boy.
How dare he smile, jiggling his goodies

in that tiny shiny bag, his black paw crinkling it,
how dare he tinkle their laughter at you.

Here's a fine basket of riddles:
If a mouth shoots off and no one's around
to hear it, who can say which came first—
push or shove, bang or whimper?
Which is news fit to write home about?

Aubade West

Ferguson, Missouri

Everywhere absence mocks me:
Jimmy, jettisoned like rotten fruit.
Franklin blown away.
Heat aplenty of all kinds,
especially when August blows its horn—
cops and summer and no ventilation
make piss-poor running buddies.
A day just like all the others,
me out here on the streets
skittery as a bug crossing a skillet,
no lungs big enough to strain
this scalded broth into brain and tissues,
plump my arteries, my soul . . .

Voice in my ear hissing *Go ahead, leave.*
Look around. No gates, no barbed wire.
As if I could walk on water.
As if water ever told one good truth,
lisping her lullabies as she rocks
another cracked cradle of Somalis
until it splits and she can pour
her final solution right through.
Me watching from the other side of the world,
high and dry on this street
running straight as a line of smack,
sun shouting down its glory:

No one's stopping you.
What are you waiting for?

Naji, 14. Philadelphia.

A bench, a sofa, anyplace flat—
just let me down
somewhere quiet, please,
a strange lap, a patch of grass . . .

What a fine cup of misery
I've brought you, Mama—cracked
and hissing with bees.
Is that your hand? Good, I did
good: I swear I didn't yank or glare.

If I rest my cheek on the curb, let it drain . . .

They say we bring it on ourselves
and trauma is what *they* feel
when they rage up flashing
in their spit-shined cars
shouting *who do you think you are?*
until everybody's hoarse.

I'm better now. Pounding's nearly stopped.

Next time I promise I'll watch my step.
I'll disappear before they can't
unsee me: better gone
than one more drop in a sea of red.

Ghettoland: Exeunt

follow the morning star

Tell yourself it's only a sliver of sun
burning into your chest, a cap of gold
or radiant halo justly worn by
the righteous at heart—

then take it off, stomp it, rip out the seams.

Wherever a wall goes up, it smolders.
Gate or street corner, buried canal—
you'll catch yourself before crossing,
stumble over perfectly flat stones,
skirt the worn curb to avoid a cart
rumbling past three centuries ago.

You stop to gaze at the softening sky
because there is nowhere else to look
without remembering pity and contempt,
without harboring rage.

Spring Cricket

Nobody loves me
but the spring cricket.

—Aviva, age 5

The Spring Cricket Considers the Question
of Negritude

I was playing my tunes all by myself;
I didn't know anybody else
who could play along.

Sure, the tunes were sad—
but sweet, too, and wouldn't come
until the day gave out: You know

that way the sky has of dangling
her last bright wisps? That's when
the ache would bloom inside

until I couldn't wait; I knelt down
to scrape myself clean
and didn't care who heard.

Then came the shouts and whistles,
the roundup into jars, a clamber of legs.
Now there were others: tumbled,

clouded. I didn't know their names.
We were a musical lantern;
children slept to our rasping sighs.

And if now and then one of us
shook free and sang as he climbed
to the brim, he would always

fall again. Which made them laugh
and clap their hands. At least then
we knew what pleased them,

and where the brink was.

The Spring Cricket Repudiates His Parable
of Negritude

Hell,

we just climbed. Reached the lip
and fell back, slipped

and started up again—
climbed to be climbing, sang

to be singing. It's just what we do.
No one bothered to analyze our blues

until everybody involved
was strung out or dead; to solve

everything that was happening
while it was happening

would have taken some serious opium.
Seriously: All wisdom

is afterthought, a sort of helpless relief.
So don't go thinking none of this grief

belongs to you: Even if
you don't know how it

feels to fall, you can get my drift;
and I, who live it

daily, have heard
that perfect word

enough to know just when
to use it—as in:

Oh hell. Hell, no.
No—

this is hell.

The Spring Cricket's Grievance: Little Outburst

Tired of singing for someone else.
Tired of rubbing my thighs
      to catch your ear.

When the sky falls tonight,
      I'll stand on my one
            green leaf

and it will be my time,
      my noise,
     my ecstasy.

The Spring Cricket Observes Valentine's Day

Twenty-four hours dedicated to the heart
and the heart in question a caricature
of something that never existed: half a butterfly
squeezing out of a lace-trimmed corset,
a fantasy floozy, dipped in red,
favorite color of the criminally insane.

Equally ferocious, this insistence
that love resides in the chest,
when everyone knows it pitches itself
into ether. That's why they speak of falling:
You step out without looking, and even
the best parts of you won't hold you up.

Ah! The lobed boxes, the chocolates softly
sweating in their pleated wrappers,
the flowers trussed and crackling on doorsteps!
From my shrub I watch them navigate
the handover—eyes shining, kisses—
then send out my own Valentine

into the darkening meadow: one crimped note
scratched from two back legs, a spark
rubbed to flame; all that I cannot be
yearning for wings, their glazed flight
becoming all of me—which I give to you
wherever, whoever you are.

The Spring Cricket's Discourse on Critics

Everybody's got a song
they've gotta sing.
So they say. So they
think. Everybody's got
a pair of fat thighs
they believe they can
just crush together
& crank out the golden
tunes, ye olde razzmatazz,
& the opposition will drop like—

no, I'm not going there.

I'm gonna sit here
awhile & watch the dew
drop: its letting go
so lurid a metaphor for Failure,
I can't help but take it
out of circulation. Everybody's
hungry, everybody's hunkered
in their hedges, hanging on—
in the end nothing's left
to talk about but Style.

Hip Hop Cricket

This 'hood's vast
and I'm its chief
sentinel, a natural
born horn.
I'm a clarion
nation, the itch
in heaven's
evening clothes.

Where I'm from
ain't no "my bad"—

I *am* bad: That's
truth. So pony
up, falsettoed
crotch-grabbers, you
whistling wannabes,
and listen to
what's *real*: I don't
have to touch it

to know that it's there.

Postlude

Stay by the hearth, little cricket.

Cendrillon

You prefer me invisible, no more than
a crisp salute far away from
your silks and firewood and woolens.

Out of sight, I'm merely an annoyance,
one slim, obstinate wrinkle in night's
deepening trance. When sleep fails,

you wish me shushed and back in my hole.
As usual, you're not listening: Time stops
only if you stop long enough to hear it

passing. This is my business:
I've got ten weeks left to croon through.
What you hear is a lifetime of song.

A Standing Witness

People are trapped in history
and history is trapped in them.

—*James Baldwin*

Beside the Golden Door

Prologue

Surely there must be something beautiful to smile upon—
the umbered blue edge of sky as it fades into evening,
the brusque green heave of the sea. When I
look up, surely there will be a cloud or a lone star

dangling. Truth is, the Truth has gone walking—
left her perch for the doves and ravens
to ravage, hightailed it to the hills, to the quiet
beyond rivers and trees. No matter

what ragged carnival may be thronging the streets,
what bleak homestead or plantation of sorrows
howling its dominion, Truth would say these are

arrogant times. Believers slaughter their doubters
while the greedy oil their lips with excuses
and the righteous turn merciless; the merciful, mad.

Your Tired, Your Poor . . .

FIRST TESTIMONY: *1968*

Who comforts you now that the wheel has broken?
No more princes for the poor. Loss whittling you thin.
Grief is the constant now, hope the last word spoken.

In a dance of two elegies, which circles the drain? A token
year with its daisies and carbines is where we begin.
Who comforts you now? That the wheel has broken

is Mechanics 101; to keep dreaming when the joke's on
you? Well, crazier legends have been written.
Grief is the constant now; hope, the last word spoken

on a motel balcony, shouted in a hotel kitchen. No kin
can make this journey for you. The route's locked in.
Who comforts you now that the wheel has broken

the bodies of its makers? Beyond the smoke and
ashes, what you hear rising is nothing but the wind.
Who comforts you? Now that the wheel has broken,

grief is the constant. Hope: the last word spoken.

Bridged Air

Second Testimony: *1969*

Year of the moon, year of love & music:
Everyone in batik, dripping beads & good will;
peace to the world, peace to the Universe!
Sing along, kiss a stranger; blankets quilting the hill.

Three days of music—did you really imagine
this was all the excuse you would need?
Rain be damned; rock 'n' roll in the mud!
The bread can run low, but please not the weed—

then the last one steps onstage, fringed like a wild saint.
Do you see? he pleads. A scorched sound:
Hear it? Lost in combat, blind to love—your anthem
shredding the heavens as the bombs pour down.

Giant

> *Butterfly, butterfly on the wall*
> *Can't you hear your country call?*

Black man's got no business being
both pretty and bold—with a right hook
as swift as his banter, his feet
a flurry of insults, disguised as dance.

There's a war going on, but he's having
none of it. He flicks those angry eyes,
then flings out a rhyme
quick as tossing a biscuit to a dog.

He's our homegrown warrior, America's
toffee-toned Titan; how dare he swagger
in the name of peace? No black man
strutting his minstrel ambitions

deserves those eloquent lips:
Swat him down, pin him to the mat!
On and on they mutter, hellbent on keeping
their own destiny unscathed

& brazenly manifest.

Huddle

I'm not a crook he crowed, and people believed him,
persuaded by flags and honor guard;
that he had trusted his generals' reports

did not justify terminating their trust in him,
leader of the free world balls-deep in the muck
of a war no one would claim to have started,

though everyone agreed it must be brought to an end
sooner rather than later. *By any means necessary,*
he was thinking, as he recorded another muddy deal,

then sent his plumbers out to plug the leaks.
Who wouldn't prefer to be standing high and dry
with someone else's fingers in the dike?

A little eavesdropping, a few ruffled papers
hardly constitutes a heist! Let's call it a *domestic incursion*;
and that the facts have been brought to light

means the system is working. No need for alarm:
A crook is just a bend in the road not yet traveled—
he's simply waiting for the smoke to clear.

Woman, Aflame

FIFTH TESTIMONY: *Roe v. Wade*

She was a mother. She was a girl who dreamed of becoming
a mother someday. She was either a tease or a tramp, a lover
or a wife—still she had to do the counting; was accused of
lacking spontaneity, being a cold-hearted bitch;
but if the days didn't add up, she'd end up
straddling a cold table in a dingy back room

or waving Goodbye Future. She was jogging. On the late shift.
Unlocking her car. And though she still remembered
the tart smack of his sweat when he held her down,
horseradish on his tongue—
none of this was she permitted to say

while lawyers argued her right to privacy, citing
statute and precedent until the court declared *Enough!*

And she and her body were free to go.

Mother of Exiles

SIXTH TESTIMONY: *The Iran Vigil*

I wish I could describe how it felt to weather
the acetylene blare of their constant labor,

the bright chatter of Industry. Each day
the next card slipped into a disappearing deck;

each night dumped its used confetti at my feet
in grim, glittering heaps. But you're not

interested. It's your turn to watch as hours
flatten into days and weeks and months

until even the staunchest among you will crumble
when you catch yourself grabbing a beer

before settling down in front of the TV
where the countdown grows. Only then, perhaps,

would you let me console you by saying
that time empties with the waiting—

though you already know this by now.

Wretched

Anywhere. Anyone. Men, boys—but women, too, and
Children, babies unborn in the womb. Doctors dispensing
Every kind of diagnosis, fear fueling rumors as the flowers
Germinate and spread, voracious; a purple hemlock
Inching trunk to collarbone, jaw to ear to eye.
Kisses sicken; loving any body but your own
May kill. Semen, needles, saliva, breast milk—
On and on the list unfurls, a dread epitaph proclaiming
Queer. Rail against the fleeing gods,
Spit into the wind; you'll tire soon enough. The worst is always
Unimaginable, though you knew well before the verdict dropped—
Weakness. Fever. Chills. Those greedy, X-rated blooms. Now
You tell *me*: What's a zero hour with no one left to count?

Limbs Astride, Land to Land

EIGHTH TESTIMONY: *The Berlin Wall*

Far away—can you hear it? Static pinging
at the edges of thought: the sound a wall makes
powering down. Can it be this easy—

one misspeak and crowds assemble;
the Evil Red Bear cuddles with the Cowboy
and Jericho topples under a jubilant swarm

of hammers chiseling for souvenirs?
Don't brood or marvel, just enjoy the music,
death strip lit for photo ops, bananas for all—

History doesn't cough up triumphs easily.
Even fear has grown tired of harboring rage
and sent it to play out in a desert

so far away, no one will notice. . . .

World-Wide Welcome

Hubba Bubba Bubble tape,
chicken pita wrap to go,
Pop Rocks, Push Pops, Dipping Dots:

Oreos!

Beanie babies by the handful,
wool or pleather, felt or straw?
Mood rings for internal weather:

Wonderbra!

Page my PalmPilot when you're done;
I'll cut through the traffic mess
and pull up curbside in my Saturn:

Thank you, GPS!

Who wouldn't want to be a Millionaire,
or a real live Princess or King of the World?
Map your genes and pierce your navel:

Spice Girl!

Fire up the circuits in your PlayStation—
if you're Game, Boy, I'll tickle your Elmo!
How's your Tamagotchi been hanging?

O, Mario!

Magic's vanished from the court,
Great Gretzky has exited the ice,
Buffy or Baywatch, Cosmo or Xena—

Reality Bites.

Gimme a logo to go with my Windows,
eBay for old, Amazon for new;
a Hubble, a Canon, an Apple a day—

and we all shout *Yahoo!*

Imprisoned Lightning

TENTH TESTIMONY: *9/11*

In cartoons, the arrow punches through
with a *poing!*—then quivers to a standstill:
our cue to laugh before Bugs or Elmer Fudd
plucks it off, and the hunt goes on.

That's how I saw it: a classic slo-mo clip,
action drawn out so it can be savored,
the target shimmering in sunlight, oblivious.

Something big was about to happen, was happening.
No one had seen this episode before
so we did nothing but stare
as the second arrow struck.

Neat. Not even a "pop"
(but who remembers listening?)—
just a delicate puff

before the world crumbled into a roar
that went on forever, blotting out all animal
comprehension—not even a thought balloon survived
to place against the bluest of mornings.

Send These to Me

Surely there can be no more princes—
yet here we are, reinventing the magic
Year of Love, though the music is scarred
and there's always a war or two going on.

At least the system seems to be working;
you've voted, done the counting, and there
he stands: America's miracle, fruit of bold dreams
and labor. Ladies and Gents, the unimaginable

is open for business! Assemble your buoyant
prophesies: Who wouldn't want to believe
in legends again, oblivious to everything except
astonishment? Well done; felicitations!

And now the story is yours.

Keep Your Storied Pomp

TWELFTH TESTIMONY: *Trump*

Granted, it felt good at first to snicker,
But now the rooster won't shut up.
How exhausting, waking to that imperious caw.

Old MacDonald's downsized to a flowerpot;
Here a body there a body sent packing,
caged—everywhere somebody muddied.

Welcome to the Age of Babble!
Here a twitter, there a tweet; a tiki torch march
back to the Good Ole Times of mayhem and murder,

hollow-points blossoming all over!
Everywhere a body bloody;
even the earth is bleeding out.

Oh indolent friends, bitter patriots:
What have you triggered that can't be undone?

The Sunset Gates

Epilogue

I didn't ask to stand under a crown of spikes
with my book and my torch, forgotten
like a lamp left burning in the corner.

My shoulder aches, my toes are throbbing.

I'd rather bathe in a park fountain
or cast benediction from the shadowy nest
of a cathedral's gilded ribs.

Liberty's pale green maiden, stranded.

Come visit! Ascend to the crown and gaze out
at the nation I've sworn to watch over.
I stand ready to tell you what I have seen.

Who among you is ready to listen?

Eight Angry Odes

Hell is empty and all the devils are here.

—*Shakespeare,* The Tempest

The Angry Odes: An Introduction

The Angry Odes are not satisfied with wonder:
birds prattle, clouds curdle then bust their guts,
mountains prefer their own splendid company.
Neither do they melt when music swells,
although they've been caught swaying
unaware, in a delicate self-embrace.

The Odes hate their names. To hell with urns
and nightingales, immortality and socks—
those artful self-immolations, pity parties
fueled by gloom or a gruff, enforced gaiety.
They snarl at affirmation, will laugh outright
when asked for declarations in return.

Do not try reason. The Odes are fed up with
misspelled signs accusing others of ignorance,
the belligerent purveyors of programmed rectitude.
Let them rage. Do your work, reap the ashes.
Perhaps they'll muster a flicker of pity,
recall a time when all they did was praise.

Pedestrian Crossing, Charlottesville

A gaggle of girls giggle over the bricks
leading off Court Square. We brake

dutifully, and wait; but there's at least
twenty of these knob-kneed creatures,

blonde and curly, still at an age that thinks
impudence is cute. Look how they dart

and dither, changing flanks as they lurch
along—golden gobbets of infuriating foolishness

or pure joy, depending on one's disposition.
At the moment mine's sour—this is taking

far too long; don't they have minders?
Just behind my shoulder in the city park

the Southern general still stands, stonewalling us all.
When I was their age I judged Goldilocks

nothing more than a pint-size criminal
who flounced into others' lives, then

assumed their clemency. Unfair,
I know, my aggression—to lump them

into a gaggle (silly geese!) when all
they're guilty of is being young. So far.

Ode on a Shopping List Found
in Last Season's Shorts

Wedged into a pocket, this folded paper scrap
has been flattened to a pink-tinged patch—
faint echo to the orange plaid cotton shorts
that even back then barely cupped my butt.

Milk tops the chart. Then bottled water,
crackers, paper towels: staples bought in bulk,
my husband's jurisdiction—meaning
we must have made several stops, together.

Then why is "Home Depot" scratched out but
not the light bulb we would have found there?
Batteries for him, styling gel for me,
emery boards, wasp spray, glycerin for shine:

What contingencies were we equipping for,
why were we running everywhere at once?
And now I see it: Ritter Sport, Almond Joy,
Mars bars and Neccos for the father

whose ravenous sweet tooth was not what finally
killed him. In the summer of that last birthday,
who could have known there would be
no more road trips to buy for, no place to go but

home? I'll never wear these shorts again.

Insomnia Etiquette

There's a movie on, so I watch it.

The usual white people
in love, distress. The usual tears.
Good camera work, though:
sunshine waxing the freckled curves
of a pear, a clenched jaw—
more tragedy, then.

I get up for some scotch and Stilton.
I don't turn on the lights.
I like moving through the dark
while the world sleeps on,
serene as a stealth bomber
nosing through clouds . . .

call it a preemptive strike,
"a precautionary measure
so sadly necessary in these perilous times."
I don't call it anything
but greediness: the weird glee
of finding my way without incident.

I know tomorrow I will regret
having the Stilton. I will regret
not being able to find
a book to get lost in,
and all those years I could get lost
in anything. Until then

it's just me and you,
Brother Night—moonless,
plunked down behind enemy lines
with no maps, no matches.
The woods deep.
Cheers.

Ode to My Right Knee

Oh, obstreperous one, ornery outside of ordinary
protocols; paramilitary probie *par*

excellence: Every evidence
you yield yells.

No noise
too tough to tackle, tears

springing such sudden salt
when walking wrenches:

Haranguer, hag, hanger-on— how
much more maddening

insidious imperfection?
Membranes matter-of-factly

corroding, crazed cartilage calmly chipping
away as another arduous ambulation

begins, bone bruising bone.
Leathery Lothario, lone laboring

gladiator grappling, groveling
for favor; fairweather forecaster, fickle friend,

jive jiggy joint:
Kindly keep kicking.

Anniversary

This is not for you, this is not a gift.
Anyways, ribbons would have been overkill.
(I thought I could make it to the store

before closing. *What kind of crap town
is this?* I shouted, kicking the locked door.)

So I messed up a little. Not that
it would've changed things if traffic had flowed
as proscribed or those knuckleheads

had learned to follow the rules:
When turning left, pull into the intersection,

use your blinkers to indicate lane change
and when merging, take turns—it's called
scissoring, dumbasses, it's also how

I made the fringe on the wrapping,
which you are permitted to appreciate

even though this is not for you.
No gifts! you said, and I got it.
I'm not stupid. I know the rules.

Shakespeare Doesn't Care

where Sylvia put her head. His Ophelia
suffered far worse, shamed by slurs, drenched
merely to advance the plot. "Buck up, Sylvia!"
he'd say. "Who needs a gloomy prince
spouting iambs while minions drag the river?
Sharpen your lead and carve us
a fresh pound of Daddy's flesh
before the rabble in the pit

starts launching tomatoes!"
Shakespeare's taking no prisoners:
he's purloined the latest gossip
to plump up his next comedy,
pens a sonnet while building
a playlist for the apocalypse.
When you gripe at reviews,
he snickers: How would you like

to be called an "upstart crow"
just because you dared write a play
instead of more "sugared sonnets"?
How's them apples next to your shriveled
sour grapes? As for the world
going to hell (alas! alack! whatever),

ditch the dramatics: He's already done
a number on that handbasket,
what with pox and the plague
bubbling up here and there,
now and then—afflictions
one could not cough away nor soothe
with piecemeal science. So chew it up
or spit it out, he might say,

although more likely he'd just shrug.
What does he care
if we all die tomorrow?
He lives in his words. You wrestle,
enraptured, with yours.
What time does with them
next, or ever after,
is someone else's rodeo.

A Sonnet for the Sonnet

You have occupied the rose-garlanded throne for so long,
no one remembers a time when love wasn't a portable feast,
metaphorical conceits sung to the gimpy tread of a heartbeat.
That true rhyme equals contentment, a neatened song

we've learned to yearn for? My Dumpling, that is
entirely your doing, a glittering *fait accompli*
we've been duped into trying to make reality, complete
with lute-plucked warbling under a moon-splashed lattice.

Let's face it: love is messy or boring or hurts like hell and then
is gone. Even when we're satisfied, beyond the garden gate
the rest waits, all those years you never thought to mention.
No matter how the cake is sliced, some choice bits break

off. It's nearly wide enough for two, this sugarcoated ledge:
We clamber on for one more lick of the jagged edge.

Little Book
of Woe

It could not be predicted. The condition had a name, the kind
of name usually associated with telethons, but the name meant
nothing . . .

—*Joan Didion,* The White Album

Illness is the most heeded of doctors: to goodness, to wisdom, we
only make promises; pain we obey.

—*Marcel Proust,* Cities of the Plain

Soup

When the doctor said *I've got good news and bad news,*
I thought of soup—how long it had been
since I had had the homemade kind,
the real deal where you soak the beans overnight
and everything is apportioned in stages:
first the onions and meat browned in oil,
then the broth added for hours of simmering,
all that saturated glistening scent stoking the house
with memories: the Jewish boy I kissed
until we both sank to our knees in the grass,
my mother's frown as she plucked weeds
from my hair—oh my mother will die from this,
my mother whose soup is the best
even though it was always oversalted because
it was labored over, it was ladled out
unconditionally, tendered sweetly
without consequences, a nonjudicial love—
and it was always soup I got first thing
in the sickbed, and there's the way tomatoes are added
at the last moment but the minor vegetables
(peas and corn and tiny diced potatoes)
come in thirty minutes before that, and how
the spices—ah, the spices—are to be doled out
sparingly, then waiting to see how strong they'd become
in the brew, their hidden aptitudes unlocked
only by time and the heat of a burbling *mélange;*
and the way my apron always got stained
but I wouldn't wash it, proud of the mess
for once, making mistakes, sloshing and dripping.

Yes, soup was what I wanted: not news
but the slow courage of the lentil
as it softened, its heart splitting into wings;
not good cop bad cop but the swift metallic smack
of too much thyme administered hastily,
the kind of mistake you never make again.
Bread, too; I wanted the whole thick crusty hump of it
laid out for vivisection (*here is my body eat*)
and lots of red wine that always feels like it's greasing my bones
with lava (*here is my blood*) . . .
and then the bad news came (who ever listens to the good?)
and before I answered, before the questions
and the arched eyebrow of my husband
standing in the doorway could fall into
pity and helplessness, I thought Yes
I'll make soup tonight, a soup fit for the gods.

Pearl on Wednesdays

"Write a poem about why people die."

Sunlight streams down on the TV Guide crossword
I fill in, even though I don't watch much TV,
so don't know Matlock's first name or
the number of seasons Studio One has aired.
My feet have chilled in their slipper socks;
I like the *not yet* thrill of completing small tasks
for a reward, as in: *Finish the puzzle before reheating
your coffee, soak your cup before going upstairs.*
You call me to the front room to show off the couch:
spray-foamed and scrubbed, it's white again after years
of lolling heads and popcorn, the bit-by-bit grime
of a family relaxing from . . . well, just living, just life.

We made these environments we cling to—
unlike the lion who accepts the zebra as meat,
or the zebra who understands he's meat
just as much or as little as he understands
the grasses he hides in or the sky's sickening lurch
when death comes. Does he fear it? You betcha.
Maybe he thinks about death all the time, too,
but I doubt it. We're the species wired for that,
and our only comfort's the world we've built
to fuss over, the props and affections
we mourn all the time we have them, practicing.
Biology is the why, Pearl. That's the easy one.

The Terror and the Pity

as in: cold pain, shitty pain,
a shock, a shirring, a ripple.

sharp, of course. more variously:
crisp or piercing, clean or fuzzy.

a whisper. a tickle cresting, then
settling down. (good.) the reliable dull roar.

sheered through. a cold punch followed
by radiating calm . . .

can it be sour? yes. salty?
perhaps; bitter, definitely;

and sweet, sweet is the worst,
a deep pure blue of an ache,

a throb caught in its own throat
trying to explain—

as in: numbing, searing, penetrating, sudden.
as in blotto. lord-have-mercy. why. please.

No Color

No dream of the ancients.

No gray, even; it's all
black or white, absence or presence

of pigment, of light . . . no matter:
They're not here, what or whoever

"they" are—the horizon's blank,
the sky a vacuum opaque

as only a vacuum can be,
decanting its endless suction.

Five p.m. I never thought
I'd find relief

in the old joke that it's always darkest
before it goes pitch black,

but at least then
it will be dark and then

thank god, black.

Blues, Straight

I ache. I ache. It's not so odd,
no rarity to find a body
going through the daily give
and take, the clarity of
blues. No reason for it:
I just find myself on pause—
paused for longer than is
proper. If I were more
seasoned, I'd ignore it.

The laws of coexistence
call for movement—through
a week, a day, a rescued instant.
One minute I'm up and running,
and then I'm not.
I smile. I nod. I practically beam.
The cup of plenty runneth
over, ruins my hands—
I've scrubbed them, but
they won't come clean.
Strange, I know, to wish
for nothing. A day
to live through. A scream.

Borderline Mambo

As if the lid stayed put on the marmalade.
As if you could get the last sip of champagne
out of the bottom of the fluted glass.
As if we weren't all dying, as if we all weren't
going to die *some* time, as if we knew for certain
when, or how. As if the baseball scores made sense
to the toddler. As if the dance steps mattered, or there's a point
where they don't. For instance wheelchair. Heart flutter.
Oxygen bottle mounted on the octogenarian's back
at the state ballroom competition—that's Manny,
still pumping the mambo with his delicious slip
of an instructor, hip hip hooray. Mambo, for instance,
if done right, gives you a chance to rest: one beat in four.
One chance in four, one chance in ten, a hundred, as if
we could understand what that means. Hooray. Keep
pumping. As if you could keep the lid on a secret
once the symptoms start to make sense. A second
instance, a respite. A third. Always that hope.
If we could just scrape that last little bit
out, if only it wouldn't bottom out
before they can decode the message
sent to the cells. Of course it matters when, even though
(because?) we live in mystery. For instance
Beauty. Love. Honor. As if we didn't like
secrets. Point where it hurts. Of course we'll tell.

Voiceover

Impossible to keep a landscape in your head.
Try it: All you'll get is pieces—the sun
emerging from behind the mountain ridge,
smoke coming off the ice on a thawing lake.
It's as if our heads can't contain
anything that vast: It just leaks out.

You can be inside a house and still feel
the rooms you're not in—kitchen below
and attic above, bedroom down the hall—
but you can't hold onto the sensation
of being both inside the walls
and outside *looking at* them
at the same time.

Where do we go with that?
Where does that lead us?

There are spaces for living
and spaces for forgetting.
Sometimes they're the same.
We walk back and forth without a twitch,
popping a beer, gabbing on the phone,
with only the occasional stubbed toe.

The keyhole sees nothing.
Has it always been blind?

It's like a dream where a voice whispers
Open your mouth and you do,
but it's not your mouth anymore
because now you're all throat,

a tunnel skewered by air.
So you rewind; and this time
when you open wide, you're standing
outside your skin, looking down
at the damage, leaning in close . . .
about to dive back into your body—
and then you wake up.

Someone once said: There are no answers,
just interesting questions.
(*Which way down?* asked the dove,
dropping the olive branch.)

If you think about it,
everything's inside something else;
everything's an envelope
inside a package in a case—

and pain knows a way into every crevice.

Rosary

I.

1 tablet	1 drop
1 tablet	1 drop

1 g	1 ml
Apply	Inject

0.5 tablet   1 tablet
      1.5 tablets

1 tablet	1 drop
1 tablet	1 drop

Use as directed

II.

Take Use Place Inject
Place Place Take Take
Apply Place Apply Take
Place Place Take Take

III.

By mouth. Into both eyes. As directed.
Into the skin. On light spots.
Vaginally. Topically.
Both eyes
By mouth
By mouth

IV.

2 times a day. 3 times. Every 6 hours.
On Monday, Wednesday, and Friday.
Daily.
Nightly.
With breakfast.
Daily for six weeks, take weekends off.
2 times daily for 3 days. For 10 days.
2 times daily. Every day.
As needed.

Green Koan

That the mind can go
wherever it wishes
is a kindness
we've come to rely on;
that it returns
unbidden to the soul
it could not banish
and learns to thrive there
is life's stubborn mercy—given
to soften or harden us,
as we choose.

Last Words

I don't want to die in a poem
the words burning in eulogy
the sun howling *why*
the moon sighing *why not*

I don't want to die in bed
which is a poem gone wrong
a world turned in on itself
a floating navel of dreams

I won't meet death in a field
like a dot punctuating a page
it's too vast yet too tiny
everyone will say it's a bit cinematic

I don't want to pass away in your arms
those gentle parentheses
nor expire outside of their swoon
self propelled   determined   shouting

let the end come
as the best parts of living have come
unsought & undeserved
inconvenient

now that's a good death

what nonsense you say
that's not even worth
writing down

This Is the Poem I Did Not Write

while sorting mail, responding to posts.
Chasing a dream I can't quite remember,
remembering things I never dreamed
could happen. Putting on rice, the laundry,
all the times it was time for pills or injections,
mounting the elliptical: stairs up, stairs down.
One martini late in the day. Writing other poems—
less impatient ones, better behaved.

Rive d'Urale

Cedar Waxwing

> I am not a poem, not
> a song, unsuspecting.
> I am not a river, exactly.
> I am not a stunned head on the wall . . .
>
> Pleasure arrives on wings of glass
> and I pay with my red bead.

The Study

> in the luminous wood the gay sparrow
> in the middle of the afternoon a white room
>
> too much paradise
>
> I do not want to go out
> I do not wish to stay in
> shining grove
> green sparrow
>
> the face a dream before it reaches the mirror

One in the Palm

> The bird?
> The bird was
> brown, not golden,

smoothed feathers in no wind.
Stilled, not still.
Stilled at the end of the seeing.

A brown ordinariness.
A cup of coffee.

Dying occurs
elsewhere, more quickly
than we in a lifetime
can imagine.

No angels.
A cup of coffee
and a bead of red:
perfect coherence.

The March of Progress

The wall went up sleekly,
no hillside.
The wall went up like a bullet,
magnificent.
The wall was recognized officially
for its achievement, the wall
slithered towards heaven on a glycerin pulley,
efficient silicone.
The wall would be so kind as to let in
Light.

Fingertip Thoughts

Sehr geehrte Zuschauer, do not believe
what you see before you: The very eyeball can deceive.
Somewhere in the picture
there is a bird, but not where
you'd have it. Also
a banner, presupposing a breeze.

Red-tipped birds from wet branches
singing, skimming the available light
into a cup. Snatch up for an instant
the dark shawl . . .

What is the spirit?
The age's slow exhalation.
What bird is that singing
beyond my window,
small skull grinning through the leaves?

Assassinated Storylines

It begins with a bird who has something
to offer—a plump one, maligned,
whose plumage has grown sooty
along the beggar's path to the city.

Talon-clutch, blue bone ring:
a scrap of color—go on,
take it, pluck it away! There.
Patience: The song is rising.

Rive d'Urale

    that which is cut out
    that which is ravaged
    that which has opened itself before the rippling blade

    that which loiters
    that which roves town to town
    abundant
    loosening

    that which burrows
    that which unlocks stone
    waters rising
    birds circling

    too many cracks to think about along this spine
    each step
    a bead

Mercy

An absolute sound,
this soughing above
the tops of trees.
For the longest while
I couldn't look up, so much
did I long to see ocean,
rough and whitened.

Such soft ululations,
such a drumroll of feathers!
Yet it was no other weather
than Wind. I looked up; the sky
lay blue as always, Biblical
and terrifying, just where
it was supposed to be.

Wayfarer's Night Song

Above the mountaintops
all is still.
Among the treetops
you can feel
barely a breath—
birds in the forest, stripped of song.
Just wait: before long
you, too, shall rest.

Johann Wolfgang von Goethe, 1776

Notes

Time's Arrow

"Bellringer": Henry Martin was born into slavery at Monticello outside of Charlottesville, Virginia, on the day Thomas Jefferson died—July 4, 1826. He rang the Rotunda bell at Jefferson's University (the University of Virginia) for over fifty years.

"From the Sidelines": A Golden Shovel inspired by Gwendolyn Brooks's poem "Notes from the Childhood and the Girlhood" *[11: my own sweet good]*. The end words are taken from the line "You kiss all the great-lipped girls that you can."

"Found Sonnet: The Wig": All terms were taken from catalog and display descriptions of actual wigs.

"A·wing'": The epigraph is from Hugo von Hofmannsthal's libretto for Richard Strauss's opera *Der Rosenkavalier.*

After Egypt

In 1516, the Jews of Venice had to move to a section of the principality known as the Ghetto—the first use of this word for segregated, and subpar, living quarters. In preparation for the 500th anniversary of this event, Università Ca' Foscari Venezia and Beit Venezia invited a number of artists, writers and intellectuals to reflect on the evolution of the word "ghetto" and its connotations and symbolism. Thanks to this project, called "Reimagining the Ghetto of Venice," and its director Shaul Bassi, I spent a month in *La Serenissima*, overlooking the Canale Grande from a magnificent apartment in the Palazzo Malipiero, the very building where a young Giacomo Casanova began solidifying his scandalous reputation.

"Foundry": *Ghetto* is a derivation of *ghet*, Venetian dialect for *foundry*, and refers to the island where foundry slag was dumped before the Jews were forced to move there.

Although just fourteen of her poems have survived (plus two letters and a manifesto), we know that Sarra Copia Sullam (1592–1641) played a pivotal role in the intellectual and cultural life of Jewish Venice. As a patron of the arts, she ran a literary salon and maintained lively correspondences with writers beyond her enclave, Jewish and Christian alike.

"Sarra's Answer": In response to Gabriele Zinano's sonnet "To a Jewess Called Signora Sarra Copia Who Loved the Virtues of Signor Anselmo Ceba Though He Is Dead"—in which Zinano praises her Christian mentor and exhorts her to convert to Christianity— Sarra composed her own sonnet, using his end words. I have attempted the same in English.

"Sarra's Blues": Sarra spent her entire life in the Ghetto of Venice. Several times during her literary career, she needed to defend herself against those she'd once considered mentors— men who attempted to discredit her accomplishments and impugn her faith. One teacher even ran an elaborate scam to extract gifts and money from his munificent pupil.

"Aubade: The Constitutional": Rabbi, scholar and writer Leone da Modena aka Leon Modena (1571–1648) was a close friend of the Sullam family.

"Transit": The speaker is the pianist Alice Herz-Sommer (1903–2014), survivor of the Theresienstadt concentration camp.

"Youth Sunday": The Sixteenth Street Baptist Church in Birmingham, Alabama, was bombed by members of the local Ku Klux Klan on the morning of September 15, 1963, killing four African-American girls and injuring fourteen other people.

Spring Cricket

"Postlude": The quote is from Jules Massenet's 1899 opera *Cendrillon* ("reste au foyer, petit grillon") and refers to the Charles Dickens novella *The Cricket on the Hearth*.

A Standing Witness

In 2017, the composer Richard Danielpour approached me with the daunting yet intriguing proposal to collaborate on a song cycle, bearing witness to the last fifty-odd years of American history. The poems in this section are my contribution to the collaboration with Danielpour and Copland House in Peekskill, New York, that became *A Standing Witness*. The world premiere had been planned for the 2020 Tanglewood Music Festival in Massachusetts, to be followed by a number of performances at other venues, including the Kennedy Center in Washington, DC, sung by mezzo-soprano Susan Graham; due to the Coronavirus pandemic all those presentations had to be postponed.

The titles for the testimonies have been plucked from Emma Lazarus's sonnet "The New Colossus," inscribed on the pedestal of the Statue of Liberty.

"Beside the Golden Door": Overview of the beauty and misery that has been the history of America. The speaker identifies herself as a witness and nothing more.

"Your Tired, Your Poor . . .": Two assassinations. The Democratic National Convention. Social crisis. The Vietnam War crescendos.

"Bridged Air": Moon landing. Woodstock. Jimi Hendrix plays the Star-Spangled Banner at the end of the festival.

"Giant": Bombing of Cambodia. Muhammad Ali refuses to be enlisted.

"Huddle": Richard Nixon, Watergate. The Vietnam War winds down.

"Woman, Aflame": *Roe v. Wade*—a seemingly decisive women's rights victory.

"Mother of Exiles": The hostage crisis in Iran shakes a nation. Vigil.

"Wretched": The AIDS epidemic, and America's reaction to it.

"Limbs Astride, Land to Land": The Soviet Union crashes—and with it the Berlin Wall. First Gulf War.

"World-Wide Welcome": An epidemic of greed. Technology takes a leap; news and information accumulation speeds up. "Can I have some more, sir?"

"Imprisoned Lightning": Fall of the Twin Towers, and the second war in Iraq.

"Send These to Me": Barack Obama. The reemergence of the American Dream.

"Keep Your Storied Pomp": Donald Trump. The rise of neo-fascism in America. The war on immigrants. The media demonized.

"The Sunset Gates": Our standing witness finally identifies herself.

Eight Angry Odes

"Ode to My Right Knee": Challenged by my students to assign myself a poetry exercise as wild as the ones I'd given them, this is what I came up with: Write a poem in which each line is dedicated to a different letter of the alphabet—that is, the line must use only words starting with that letter. Although the selection of letters and their order was open, it was a doozy nevertheless!

Little Book of Woe

On December 7, 1997, I woke up, stepped in the shower, and discovered that I was numb from the chest down. It took a few terrifying years before the cavalcade of bizarre, shifting symptoms manifested into a clear diagnosis: Relapsing-Remitting Multiple Sclerosis. Early predictions were dire, envisaging progressive immobility and a wheelchair-bound future. But I was lucky. Although I struggled with increasing fatigue and lost feeling in my extremities—which made writing by hand harder and harder and playing the cello and my beloved viola da gamba impossible—pharmaceutical science came to the rescue. While I floundered between alternating bouts of fear and depression, my husband researched treatment options and suggested I opt for a drug that had only recently been approved. I will forever be grateful to my medical team at the University of Virginia for being game to try what then was less proven. As the years scrolled by, the frequency and severity of my relapses wondrously diminished, symptoms began to flatten out, and MRI scans verified that the improvements I was experiencing were real. All this time I hid what was happening to me from the public—first and foremost to spare my aging parents, but also because I needed to become acquainted with the new me before other people weighed in; the last thing the poet in me wanted was pity. So I kept traveling all over the world with my husband always near, just in case. I relearned walking steadily through ballroom dancing, which taught me how numb toes could gauge balance by how much pressure was exerted on the floor; I got stumbling under control. I stopped pushing myself to do everything for everyone. I'm still figuring out how to compose poems on the keyboard but have been able to resort to some handwriting again. Nowadays, after over two decades with MS, the sword above my head seems blunted enough that I often forget it's still there; the sting of my nightly injections is a small price to pay for having a semblance of my old healthy life back.

"Rive d'Urale": In 1989, that year's fellows at the National Humanities Center in Research Triangle Park, North Carolina, commissioned a collaborative work from me and Polish artist Ewa Kuryluk. Ewa designed a permanent installation featuring two scrolls, one vertical with her red drawing, and one horizontal with my poem. The title "Rive d'Urale"— French for "at the outskirts of the Ural"—came from rearranging the letters in our names and alludes to the political unrest growing in that region at the time. A few months later, the Berlin Wall fell.

Acknowledgments

American Poetry Review: "Declaration of Interdependence"; "Ode on a Shopping List Found in Last Season's Shorts"; "The Terror and the Pity"; "This is the Poem I Did Not Write"

American Scholar: "No Color"

The Believer: "Hip Hop Cricket"; "The Spring Cricket's Discourse on Critics"

The Black Scholar: "Elevator Man, 1949"

Callaloo: "Family Reunion" (as "Reunion, 2005"); "Rive d'Urale"; "Scarf" (in slightly different form)

Chicago Quarterly Review: "Climacteric"; "Shakespeare Doesn't Care"

Connotation Press: "Anniversary"

CUE—A Journal of Prose Poetry: "Prose in a Small Space"

Georgia Review: "Aubade: The Constitutional"; "Aubade East"; "Aubade West"; "Ghettoland: Exeunt"; "Lucille, Post-Operative Years"

Harvard Review: "The Angry Odes: An Introduction"; "Eurydice, Turning"; "Rosary"

Iowa Review: "Blues, Straight"; "Green Koan"; "A Sonnet for the Sonnet"; "The Spring Cricket's Grievance"

Kenyon Review: "Island"; "Soup"; "The Spring Cricket Observes Valentine's Day"

The New York Times Sunday Magazine: "Youth Sunday"

The New Yorker: "Bellringer"; "Found Sonnet: The Wig"; "Last Words"; "Pedestrian Crossing, Charlottesville"; "The Spring Cricket Considers the Question of Negritude"; "Vacation"; "Wayfarer's Night Song"

Orion: "Pearl on Wednesdays"

Paris Review: "Naji, 14. Philadelphia."; "Postlude"

Ploughshares: "Mercy"

Poem-a-Day: "Borderline Mambo"; "Trans-"; "Transit"; "Your Tired, Your Poor . . ." (as "Testimony: 1968")

Poet Lore: "The Spring Cricket Repudiates His Parable of Negritude"

Poetry: "Mirror"; "Voiceover"

The Root: "Trayvon, Redux"

Slate: "Insomnia Etiquette"

Virginia Quarterly Review: "Ode to My Right Knee"

"A·wing′" first appeared in *Something Understood*, ed. Stephen Burt and Nick Halpern, University of Virginia Press, 2009.

Much of the section **After Egypt** ("Foundry"; "Sarra's Answer"; "Sarra's Blues"; "Aubade: The Constitutional"; "Sketch for Terezín"; "Orders of the Day"; "Transit"; "Aubade East"; "Trayvon, Redux"; "Aubade West"; "Ghettoland: Exeunt") appeared as "Reimagining the Ghetto" in *Poems for Sarra / Poesie per Sara* (Damocle Edizioni, Venice, Italy, 2018).

"Girls on the Town, 1946" was commissioned by The Academy of American Poets and The New York Philharmonic as part of their *Project 19* initiative.

"Youth Sunday" was commissioned for the special issue of *The New York Times Sunday Magazine* that evolved into The 1619 Project.

"Orders of the Day" and "Sketch for Terezín" originally appeared in *Liberation: New Works on Freedom from Internationally Renowned Poets,* ed. Mark Ludwig (Beacon Press, 2015).

A Standing Witness: A collaboration commissioned by Copland House in Peekskill, New York, the 14 poems comprising this lyric sequence have been set to music by composer Richard Danielpour and are scheduled to be premiered by mezzo-soprano Susan Graham in 2021/22.

Heartfelt gratitude goes to Jill Bialosky for her part in shepherding this book into the world. Thanks to Aviva Dove-Viebahn for being a stimulating sounding board as well as an ever-smart daughter. As for Fred Viebahn, my around-the-clock confidante and midnight editor—there aren't words enough to sing his praises and my love, again and again.